THE ULTIMATE
BOSTON BRUINS
TRIVIA BOOK

A Collection of Amazing Trivia Quizzes
and Fun Facts for Die-Hard Bruins Fans!

Ray Walker

Exclusive Free Book

Crazy Sports Stories

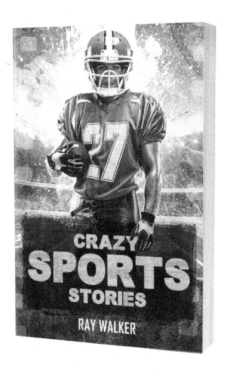

As a thank you for getting a copy of this book I would like to offer you a free copy of my book Crazy Sports Stories which comes packed with interesting stories from your favorite sports such as Football, Hockey, Baseball, Basketball and more.

Grab your free copy over at
RayWalkerMedia.com/Bonus

CONTENTS

INTRODUCTION

Team fandom should be inspirational. Our attachment to our favorite teams should fill us with pride, excitement, loyalty, and a sense of fulfillment in knowing that we are part of a community with many other fans who feel the same way.

Boston Bruins fans are no exception. With a long, rich history in the NHL, the Bruins have inspired their supporters for nearly a century with their tradition of colorful players, memorable eras, big moves, and unique moments.

This book is meant to be a celebration of those moments and an examination of the collection of interesting, impressive, or important details that allow us to understand the full stories behind the players and the team.

You may use the book as you wish. Each chapter contains twenty quiz questions in a mixture of multiple choice, true or false formats, an answer key (Don't worry, it's on a separate page!), and a section of ten "Did You Know" factoids about the team.

Some readers will use this book to test themselves with the quiz questions. How much Bruins history did you really know? How many of the finer points can you remember?

Some will use it competitively (Isn't that the heart of sports?), waging contests with friends and fellow devotees, to see who can lay claim to being the biggest fan.

Some will enjoy it as a learning experience, gaining insight to enrich their fandom and adding color to their understanding of their favorite team.

Still others may use it to teach, sharing the wonderful anecdotes inside to inspire a new generation of fans to hop aboard the Bruins bandwagon.

Whatever your purpose may be, we hope you enjoy delving into the amazing background of The Big, Bad Bruins!

Oh…and for the record, information and statistics in this book are current up to the beginning of 2020. The Bruins will surely topple more records and win more awards as the seasons pass, so keep this in mind when you're watching the next game with your friends, and someone starts a conversation with "Did you know…?".

CHAPTER 1:

ORIGINS & HISTORY

QUIZ TIME!

1. In which year were the Boston Bruins founded?

    a. 1910

    b. 1914

    c. 1920

    d. 1924

2. Boston is the NHL's oldest surviving American franchise.

    a. True

    b. False

3. The Bruins are considered an "Original Six" team, along with each other team below except for which one?

    a. Detroit Red Wings

    b. Montreal Canadiens

    c. Montreal Maroons

    d. New York Rangers

4. Who was the founder of the Boston Bruins?

    a. Charles Adams

b. Tom Yawkey

c. Jason Jacobs

d. Patrick O'Sullivan

5. How much was the franchise fee for the original rights to Boston's NHL team?

a. $500

b. $5,000

c. $15,000

d. $50,000

6. Why was the team given the name Bruins?

a. There was a prevalence of bears in the nearby forests of Massachusetts.

b. It exemplified qualities desired in the players; speed, agility, power, and cunning.

c. It played on "brewing," an industry that was both famous and popular in Boston.

d. It followed the alliteration used by the town's baseball team, the Braves.

7. Montreal Canadiens owner George Kennedy offered to buy and shut down the Bruins after their first season, because he did not enjoy travelling to Boston.

a. True

b. False

8. Which team did Boston face in its first ever NHL game (which resulted in a 2-1 Boston victory)?

a. Toronto Maple Leafs

b. New York Rangers

c. Montreal Maroons

d. Chicago Blackhawks

9. Which player scored the first ever goal for the Boston Bruins?

   a. Eddie Shore

   b. Smokey Harris

   c. Dit Clapper

   d. Walt Johnson

10. From which league did the Bruins obtain their first ever "superstar" player, defenseman Eddie Shore?

    a. The Western Hockey League

    b. The American Hockey League

    c. The Quebec Major Junior Hockey League

    d. The North Eastern Hockey Association

11. How did Boston fare in its first ever playoff run?

    a. Lost in the first round

    b. Lost in the semifinal

    c. Lost in the final

    d. Won the Stanley Cup

12. The Bruins' long-time home, Boston Garden, was built by the same entrepreneur who built Madison Square Garden in New York City.

    a. True

    b. False

13. Boston Garden was built for how much, and stood for 70 years, housing the Bruins, Celtics, and many other events?

   a. $10 thousand
   b. $100 thousand
   c. $1 million
   d. $10 million

14. In which year did the Bruins win their first Stanley Cup?

   a. 1927
   b. 1929
   c. 1933
   d. 1935

15. What winning percentage did the 1929-30 Bruins record, making it an NHL record for best regular season, that still stands?

   a. .800
   b. .850
   c. .875
   d. .900

16. Original Bruins GM Art Ross invented mesh goalie nets, beveled pucks, and a skate guard to protect the Achilles tendon.

   a. True
   b. False

17. WBZ Radio broadcasted the earliest Boston Bruins games, with who as their play-by-play announcer?

   a. Ryan Frank

b. Matthew O'Donnell

c. Frank Ryan

d. Bob Wilson

18. Crafty GM Art Ross was the first ever in the NHL to use which of the following strategies?

a. Telling a player to fake an injury in order to buy time for his team to rest

b. Turning the heat up 10 degrees higher in the visitor's locker room

c. Creating a "one-timer" by shooting a passed puck before stopping it

d. Pulling the goalie to use an extra attacking skater

19. In their first 15 years of existence, how many times did the Bruins finish in first place in their division?

a. 2

b. 4

c. 6

d. 8

20. Boston's early success led to an offer from oil tycoon John D. Rockefeller to purchase the team and move it to his home in upstate New York.

a. True

b. False

QUIZ ANSWERS

1. D – 1924

2. A – True

3. C – Montreal Maroons

4. A – Charles Adams

5. C – $15,000

6. B – It exemplified qualities desired in the players; speed, agility, power, and cunning.

7. B – False

8. C – Montreal Maroons

9. B – Smokey Harris

10. A – The Western Hockey League

11. C – Lost in the final

12. A – True

13. D – $10 million

14. B – 1929

15. C – .875

16. A – True

17. C – Frank Ryan

18. D – Pulling the goalie to use an extra attacking skater

19. C – 6

20. B – False

DID YOU KNOW?

1. The Bruins first played in Boston Arena, where they skated for four years. This building, which has now been taken over by Northeastern University and renamed Matthews Arena, is the oldest existing building still used to play ice hockey today.

2. Although Charles Adams owned the team, General Manager Art Ross, who had been well-known as a player, became the team's public face for its first three decades in the league.

3. Boston, hamstrung in its inaugural season by regional rights for clubs to obtain players, finished with a 6-24 record. This .200 winning percentage is still a franchise record for worst performance in a season.

4. In their second year of existence, the Bruins improved. Other expansion teams proved easier to beat, and the Bruins were competitive, missing the playoffs by a single point.

5. The first hockey game in venerable Boston Garden was held on November 20, 1928. Fans flocked to the arena to see Boston face Montreal, and over 2,000 people without tickets snuck in to watch the game.

6. At the time Boston Garden was built, the NHL did not have a standard rink size. As a result, for many decades, its ice surface was both shorter (by 9 feet) and narrower (by 2 feet) than other rinks.

7. Those travelling to watch the Bruins during the twentieth century did not have to worry much about parking. The Bruins played on top of North Station, a subway stop that carried many spectators to and from the games.

8. Organist John Kiley provided the soundtrack to early Bruins games. He was known as the answer to the trivia question "Name the only man to play for the Celtics, Bruins, *and* Red Sox."

9. Legendary tough guy Eddie Shore once missed a Bruins train to Montreal. He drove himself there through a snowstorm, arriving with frostbite, and proceeded to score the game-winning goal.

10. In March of 1933, the Bruins won the only forfeited contest in NHL history. Angry after one disputed goal, Blackhawks coach Tommy Gorman refused to let his players continue, and Boston was given the victory.

CHAPTER 2:

JERSEYS & NUMBERS

QUIZ TIME!

1. In which year did the team's colors change from brown and yellow to black and gold?

    a. 1928
    b. 1935
    c. 1948
    d. 1958

2. Before their famous block "B," the Bruins used a bear paw with claws as the logo on their jerseys.

    a. True
    b. False

3. Not counting 0, how many single digit numbers are still in circulation and have NOT been retired by the Bruins?

    a. 0
    b. 1
    c. 2
    d. 3

4. Which player competed for the Bruins for just nine seasons; the shortest tenure of anyone whose number has been retired by the franchise?

    a. Bobby Orr
    b. Lionel Hitchman
    c. Cam Neely
    d. Phil Esposito

5. Marc Savard is the only Bruin to ever wear which uniform number?

    a. 91
    b. 93
    c. 97
    d. 00

6. Which jersey number has been worn by 37 players, more than any other number?

    a. 7
    b. 9
    c. 29
    d. 31

7. For a few seasons, Boston wore a football style jersey with sweater numbers on the front instead of the usual team logo.

    a. True
    b. False

8. In which year were players' name plates first added to the backs of their jerseys?

a. 1939

b. 1945

c. 1952

d. 1977

9. Bobby Orr is famously known as "Number Four, Bobby Orr." What jersey number did he wear in his first pre-season with the club, before settling into the iconic 4?

a. 9

b. 27

c. 18

d. 36

10. The Bruins' "spoked B" logo first appeared in which season?

a. 1938-39

b. 1948-49

c. 1958-59

d. 1968-69

11. Who is the most recent Bruin to have his number retired by the club?

a. Adam Oates

b. Cam Neely

c. Ray Bourque

d. Rick Middleton

12. During the 1970s, the Bruins experimented occasionally with wearing Cooperalls—full hockey pants—as part of their uniform.

a. True

b. False

13. Which Bruins player overlooked superstition and wore the unlucky number 13 for five seasons?

   a. Johnny Bucyk

   b. Wayne Cashman

   c. Ken Linseman

   d. Al Iafrate

14. For how many seasons did the Bruins sweaters feature laces on them?

   a. 1

   b. 7

   c. 10

   d. 17

15. Who is the only Bruins player with a retired number who played both forward and defense for the team?

   a. Eddie Shore

   b. Lionel Hitchman

   c. Dit Clapper

   d. Milt Schmidt

16. No Bruin has ever worn a number over 92 in a regular season game.

   a. True

   b. False

17. Bruins GM Harry Sinden claimed for years that this other franchise stole the Bruins design and colors.

a. Pittsburgh Penguins

b. Pittsburgh Steelers

c. Pittsburgh Pirates

d. Las Vegas Golden Knights

18. Equipment manager Keith Robinson says "people avoid it" about which Boston jersey number, that is supposed to be cursed?

a. 0

b. 13

c. 93

d. 6

19. Longtime Bruins defenseman and captain Zdeno Chara wore number 3 in Ottawa and New York before coming to Boston, where it was retired. What number did he choose instead?

a. 6

b. 13

c. 30

d. 33

20. No Bruins skater has ever worn number 30, because the Bruins unofficially reserve that number for goaltenders.

21. True

22. False

QUIZ ANSWERS

1. B – 1935

2. B – False

3. C – 2

4. D – Phil Esposito

5. A – 91

6. C – 29

7. A – True

8. D – 1977

9. B – 27

10. B – 1948-49

11. D – Rick Middleton

12. B – False

13. C – Ken Linseman

14. B – 7

15. C – Dit Clapper

16. A – True

17. A – Pittsburgh Penguins

18. D – 6

19. D – 33

20. B – False

DID YOU KNOW?

1. Boston's original colors, brown and yellow, were chosen to match the colors of Finast (short for First National Stores, Inc.), a grocery store chain that Bruins founder Charles Adams also owned.

2. Bruins captain Ray Bourque chose his unusual number, 77, out of respect for former Bruin Phil Esposito. Both had worn number 7, and Bourque agreed to change to 77 so Boston could retire Esposito's jersey.

3. Jersey number 89 has been worn for the fewest games in Bruins history. Left winger Zdenek Blatny wore it for just five games during the 2005-2006 season.

4. Despite having ten Vezina Trophy winners in franchise history, the Boston Bruins have never retired a goalie's jersey or number.

5. Enforcer Terry O'Reilly had his number 24 retired in 2002 after spending thirteen seasons with the Bruins. They raised his number to the rafters, appropriately, on October 24.

6. The spoked B in Boston's logo is a reference to the city's nickname as "The Hub." It was introduced for the team's 25th anniversary season.

7. Bruins defender Brandon Carlo originally wore number 26, for his birthday, but switched to 25 when it became available, because he thought Christmas was even better.

8. When the Bruins moved to a new arena in 1995, they also debuted the "Pooh Bear" jersey—a gold base with a brown bear's head as the logo on the front.

9. No player on the Bruins has ever worn 0 or 00 as his uniform number.

10. Between 2008-2016, Boston sported a unique "Men in Black" third jersey, with a V-neck, retro bear logo, spoked B shoulder patch, and no stripes at the bottom.

CHAPTER 3:

FAMOUS QUOTES

QUIZ TIME!

1. Which Bruins coach was quoted as saying, "When I was a kid, I used to pray to the Lord to make me a hockey player. But I forgot to mention the NHL, so I spent 16 years in the minors."

   a. Claude Julien
   b. Lynn Patrick
   c. Pat Burns
   d. Don Cherry

2. Bruins legend Lionel Hitchman believed in the restorative power of road trips so much that he once remarked, "Sometimes all you need to feel better is a winning streak and a full tank of gas."

   a. True
   b. False

3. Which Bruin said, after being eliminated from the Stanley Cup playoffs, "The remedy, right now, is two scotches and an aspirin."?

a. Derek Sanderson

b. Milan Lucic

c. Harry Sinden

d. Ted Donato

4. Hall of Fame defenseman Bobby Orr once said the key to hockey was to "forget about style; worry about _____."

a. Substance

b. Scoring

c. Your team

d. Results

5. Though he played well at Walpole High School in Massachusetts and loved the Boston Bruins, this future Bruin said that, at the time, "I never allowed myself the fantasy of playing for that team."

a. Mike Milbury

b. Bill Guerin

c. Steve Kasper

d. Jim Craig

6. In 1967, which opposing player correctly predicted the future when he commented, "I'm just glad I won the Norris Trophy now, because I expect it's going to belong to Bobby Orr from now on."? Orr would win the next eight consecutive trophies.

a. Pierre Pilote

b. Harry Howell

c. Tim Horton

d. Doug Mohns

7. Brash Bruins player Leo Labine refused to back down from anyone, even fiery Maurice Richard. Once when Richard speared him with a stick, Labine retorted, "Look, Rocket, you've got 32 teeth. Do you want to try for 16?"

   a. True
   b. False

8. Agitator Brad Marchand prompted an unusual comment from which famous basketball player, who said of watching the Bruins forward: "That little Marchand dude, he makes me want to punch him in the face sometimes." Which basketball player was this?

   a. Bill Laimbeer
   b. Larry Bird
   c. Draymond Green
   d. Charles Barkley

9. Who said, jokingly, after assisting on the celebrated goal in which Bobby Orr flies through the air, when scoring against the St. Louis Blues in the Stanley Cup Final, "I made the kid famous!"?

   a. Derek Sanderson
   b. Phil Esposito
   c. Wayne Cashman
   d. Stan Jonathan

10. A Bruins coach once enthused about the body-checking talents of which one of his players, stating, "I used to describe it as being hit with a bag of cement."

a. Lyndon Byers

b. Johnny Bucyk

c. Zdeno Chara

d. Milan Lucic

11. Which mathematically challenged Bruins player remarked after a loss: "It's an 82-game season. We weren't going to go 80-3, or whatever it was."

   a. Peter McNab

   b. Mike Knuble

   c. Gary Galley

   d. Brett Richie

12. Although NHL players rarely complain in public about a teammate, the rift between Boston's Brad Park and Johnny McKenzie did spill over into the media, as McKenzie said, "I hated sharing a dressing room with that creep!".

   a. True

   b. False

13. Which team did legendary defenseman Ray Bourque get traded to (and win the Stanley Cup with), before gushing about Boston immediately in the aftermath of the win: "The fans, I can't thank them enough for their support, and it is going to be unbelievable going back there this summer!"

   a. Colorado Avalanche

   b. Detroit Red Wings

   c. New Jersey Devils

   d. Dallas Stars

14. During a tense playoff series, Bruins goalie Tim Thomas memorably said about which opposing goalie: "I didn't realize it was my job to pump his tires."?

    a. Braden Holtby
    b. Roberto Luongo
    c. Sergei Bobrovsky
    d. Martin Brodeur

15. Playing in an era without cages, visors, or even helmets, which Bruin commented on the dangers of hockey by saying: "We get nose jobs all the time in the NHL, and we don't even have to go to the hospital."

    a. Stan Jonathan
    b. Don Sweeney
    c. Brad Park
    d. Busher Jackson

16. Current Bruins superstar Patrice Bergeron is humble about his skills, and once told an interviewer: "Eddie Shore and those guys back in the Original Six Days...*they* had the skills! I would have been lucky to have been a fourth liner on those teams!".

    a. True
    b. False

17. To whose slick moves was a Bruins teammate referring when he claimed in 1974: "You could take anyone in the league, give _____ the puck and 90-percent of the time he'd turn the other guy inside out."

a. Bobby Orr

b. Phil Esposito

c. Rick Middleton

d. Jean Ratelle

18. Which coach had a soothing manner with young goalies, telling Byron Dafoe after giving up six goals in a game: "Do you see that yellow star up there? That's the sun and it came out today. Don't worry about it; you're going back into the nets."?

a. Pat Burns

b. Robbie Ftorek

c. Steve Kasper

d. Mike Keenan

19. Often-injured Bruins forward Cam Neely never let his injuries become an excuse. He claimed: "Pain is nothing. Pain is in the mind. _____"

a. Get over it!

b. I'll show them what pain really means.

c. The only real pain is losing.

d. If you can walk, you can run.

20. Bruins icon Don Cherry once referred to Winnipeg assistant coach Alpo Suhonen as: "some kind of dog food."

a. True

b. False

QUIZ ANSWERS

1. D – Don Cherry

2. B – False

3. C – Harry Sinden

4. D – Results

5. A – Mike Milbury

6. B – Harry Howell

7. A – True

8. D – Charles Barkley

9. A – Derek Sanderson

10. B – Johnny Bucyk

11. D – Brett Richie

12. A – True

13. A – Colorado Avalanche

14. B – Roberto Luongo

15. C – Brad Park

16. B – False

17. C – Rick Middleton

18. A – Pat Burns

19. D – If you can walk, you can run.

20. A – True

DID YOU KNOW?

1. During Phil Esposito's 1970s heyday, a popular bumper sticker in the Boston area proclaimed, "Jesus Saves, Esposito scores on the rebound!".

2. Asked once what he would have become had he not played hockey, Bruins winger Cam Neely replied honestly, "Petroleum distributor. It was one of my last jobs before playing hockey. Pumping gas."

3. Bruins coach Bruce Cassidy explained the mentality his team has when playing playoff games on the road thusly: "I hear people saying they come into another team's building and 'we have to weather the storm.' Well, we want to *create* the storm."

4. In 1933, the Bruins and Maple Leafs played a game in Boston so long that it lasted into the sixth overtime period. How long did it feel to the fans in attendance? Publicist Ed Fitkin wrote that by later overtimes: "morning papers appeared in the rink," which the fans read, hoping to find out the result!

5. Defenseman Brad Park, on trying to slow down high-flying Montreal Canadiens star Guy Lafleur, revealed, "We knew that he was a great player and would try to have Don Marcotte, our best checker, with him as much as possible. If Guy went for a pee, Donny was there to put the seat up!"

6. During the 2013 playoff season, Boston took a two game to none lead over the Pittsburgh Penguins. This prompted a rash of prank phone calls from Bruins fans to Pittsburgh sports bars. "Hi, is Owen there?" the fan would say. "Owen who?" was the reply from the barkeeps. "Oh and two!" came the hilarious punchline. One bar owner said, "We were really good sports about the first couple, but it's like forty times a day now."

7. Bruins coach and broadcaster Don Cherry often spoke his mind, once putting down opponent Randy Gregg, who was a doctor as well as a hockey player, for missing an empty net: "How would you like that guy operating on you with those hands?".

8. Popular Bruin Phil Esposito was told by his coach he was being traded. He replied, "Okay, but if you say New York Rangers, I'm going to jump out that window." The coach looked at his assistant and said, "Bobby, open the window."

9. Ray Bourque gave some sage advice to those looking to follow in his footsteps: "Goals live on the other side of obstacles and challenges. Be relentless in pursuit of those goals, especially in the face of obstacles. Along the way, make no excuses and place no blame."

10. Noted Bruins pest Brad Marchand was once asked by a reporter which emoji he would put on his stick. Without missing a beat, he replied, "I would never put an emoji on my stick. I have way more self-respect than that... (pause)... but I'll lick a guy."

CHAPTER 4:

CATCHY NICKNAMES

QUIZ TIME!

1. Bruins center Ken Linseman went by the nickname of which small creature?

    a. The Squirrel
    b. The Mouse
    c. The Rodent
    d. The Rat

2. Goalie Jim Carey was nicknamed "The Net Detective" as a play on words fashioned after Hollywood comedian Jim Carrey, star of a movie called *Ace Ventura: Pet Detective*.

    a. True
    b. False

3. As a result of earning shutouts in six of his initial eight starts during his rookie season, Bruins goalie Frank Brimsek picked up which nickname?

    a. The Wall
    b. Frankie Shutout

   c. Mr. Zero

   d. Blank Slate

4. Which Bruins player is known as "Jumbo" because of his size?

   a. Hal Gill

   b. Joe Thornton

   c. Bobby Bauer

   d. Zdeno Chara

5. Boston forward Terry O'Reilly's nickname came from which Looney Tunes character?

   a. Tasmanian Devil

   b. Bugs Bunny

   c. Marvin the Martian

   d. Tweety Bird

6. Towering defender Zdeno Chara is known by which literal nickname?

   a. The Tower of Power

   b. The Pillar of Defense

   c. Big Z

   d. Hulk

7. Forward Rick Middleton was nicknamed "Nifty" because he was considered the sharpest dresser on the Bruins, and always packed extra luggage for his suits on road trips.

   a. True

   b. False

8. Boston's Johnny McKenzie was known as "Pie," which was a short form of his original nickname:

   a. Pie Face
   b. The Pied Piper
   c. Pie in the Sky
   d. Slice o' Pie

9. Which of these nicknames was NOT applied to the forward line of Phil Esposito, Wayne Cashman, and Ken Hodge?

   a. The Nitro Line
   b. The Dogs of War Line
   c. The Espo Line
   d. The Three Bears Line

10. In his second season with the Bruins, forward Mel Hill scored three playoff overtime goals to knock out the New York Rangers, earning him what nickname?

    a. Hill the Thrill
    b. Mr. Clutch
    c. Sudden Death
    d. Ranger Killer

11. Fan favorite Leo Labine was known by which suitable nickname?

    a. Double L
    b. The Lion
    c. The Astronomer
    d. Punchy

12. "The Merlot Line" consisting of Daniel Paille, Shawn Thornton, and Gregory Campbell, took its name from the color of their practice sweaters, after refusing to be called the team's fourth line.

    a. True
    b. False

13. Chasing women, reckless driving, and arrests for mischief earned Bruins defenseman Al Iafrate this nickname:

    a. Casanova
    b. Wild Thing
    c. Trouble
    d. Hellraiser

14. Diminutive Boston goalie Tim Thomas was nicknamed after which children's cartoon character?

    a. Barney the Dinosaur
    b. Inspector Gadget
    c. Garfield the Cat
    d. Thomas the Tank Engine

15. "The Uke Line" consisted of two Ukrainian players, Johnny Bucyk and Vic Stasiuk. The third member, Bronco Horvath, was not actually Ukrainian but had his lineage in which country?

    a. Germany
    b. Hungary
    c. Yugoslavia
    d. Austria

16. Bruins netminder Byron Dafoe adopted a nickname based on an eighteenth century English poet and was known to fans as "Lord Byron."

    a. True
    b. False

17. Young Bruins players David Krejci, Milan Lucic, and Phil Kessel came together in 2008 to form which line?

    a. The Peach Fuzz Line
    b. The Under-Agers
    c. The Puberty Line
    d. The Grizzled Vet Line

18. Which of the following players was the "S" on the "GAS Line" of the 2000s-era Bruins, playing along with Bill Guerin and Jason Allison?

    a. Marco Sturm
    b. Marc Savard
    c. Sergei Samsonov
    d. Tyler Seguin

19. Colorful goaltender Andy Moog went by several nicknames, which of the following was he NOT known as?

    a. Peaches
    b. Mr. Kerosene
    c. Dennis the Menace
    d. Squeaky

20. Though they did not often play together, when they did, the combination of large forwards Joe Thornton, Mike

Knuble, and Glen Murray was dubbed "The 700 Pound Line."

a. True
b. False

QUIZ ANSWERS

1. D – The Rat

2. A – True

3. C – Mr. Zero

4. B – Joe Thornton

5. A – Tasmanian Devil

6. C – Big Z

7. B – False

8. A – Pie Face

9. D – The Three Bears Line

10. C – Sudden Death

11. B – The Lion

12. A – True

13. B – Wild Thing

14. D – Thomas the Tank Engine

15. B – Hungary

16. A – True

17. A – The Peach Fuzz Line

18. C – Sergei Samsonov

19. B – Mr. Kerosene

20. A – True

DID YOU KNOW?

1. Colorful Bruins coach Don Cherry earned the nickname "Grapes" because, as a player, he suited up for only one game in the NHL and was said to have "sour grapes" about it.

2. As a young rookie, Harvey Jackson was asked by a trainer to carry some sticks for his teammates. When he refused, saying he was there to play hockey, the trainer called him a "fresh busher" —a nobody recently called up from the minors. The name stuck, and he became "Busher" Jackson for the rest of his career.

3. Defender Torey Krug's scary nickname, "Freddy," was given to him because of his last name, in homage to horror villain Freddy Krueger from the popular *A Nightmare on Elm Street* series.

4. Johnny Bucyk, who spent two decades playing for the Bruins, was nicknamed "Chief" by a Boston newspaper artist who thought his features looked like he had a First Nation heritage. Despite being Ukrainian, Bucyk loved the nickname.

5. Current Bruin Patrice Bergeron lends his "Mr. Perfect" nickname to the line he centers. Also featuring wingers Brad Marchand and David Pastrnak, the trio are called "The Perfection Line."

6. Bruins winger Brad Marchand, a terrific player, but one

who often crosses the line into dirty play, has been suspended several times by the NHL. He goes by the ironic nickname "Precious Little Angel."

7. In the 1930s, the Bruins iced a forward line featuring Milt Schmidt, Bobby Bauer, and Woody Dumart. Although all three were from Kitchener, Ontario, their German heritage earned them the nickname "The Kraut Line."

8. Original Bruins superstar Eddie Shore was first known as "The Edmonton Express" when he arrived in Boston from Western Canada. Later, as a veteran with a reputation for toughness and ferocity, he became affectionately known as "Old Blood and Guts."

9. The Bruins' renowned "Dynamite Line" of the '20s and '30s featured three players who already had individual nicknames of their own: Ralph "Cooney" Weiland, James "Dutch" Gainor, and Aubrey "Dit" Clapper.

10. In the 1960s and '70s, the Bruins put together teams that were fast, tough, and successful. Their players were colorful and did not back down from anyone, on or off the ice. It was during this time period that the team became alliteratively known as "The Big, Bad Bruins."

CHAPTER 5:

THE CAPTAIN CLASS

QUIZ TIME!

1. This player was the first ever Boston Bruins player to be named captain, in 1925.

    a. Eddie Shore

    b. Hal Laycoe

    c. Sprague Cleghorn

    d. Bobby Bauer

2. The Bruins are the only franchise that has ever won a Stanley Cup in a year in which they did not name a captain.

    a. True

    b. False

3. How many players that have held the Bruins' captaincy have been elected to the Hockey Hall of Fame?

    a. 2

    b. 4

    c. 6

    d. 8

4. Which player has served the most seasons (15) as the Boston Bruins captain?

    a. Dit Clapper

    b. Ray Bourque

    c. Zdeno Chara

    d. Johnny Bucyk

5. Who was the first Bruins captain to win the Stanley Cup with the team?

    a. Sprague Cleghorn

    b. Lionel Hitchman

    c. Milt Schmidt

    d. Dit Clapper

6. This big, bad Bruin set the mark for most penalty minutes in a season by a Boston captain.

    a. Zdeno Chara

    b. Joe Thornton

    c. Terry O'Reilly

    d. Fern Flaman

7. Bitterness over not being named captain led to Phil Esposito's eventual trade from Boston to the New York Rangers.

    a. True

    b. False

8. In which year did the Bruins name their first captain who was not born in Canada?

    a. 1976

b. 1986

c. 1996

d. 2006

9. Which Bruin was the youngest player in the team's history to be made captain?

a. Rick Middleton

b. Dit Clapper

c. Jason Allison

d. Joe Thornton

10. The team has had some great leaders who were never given the formal responsibility of being the Bruins captain. Which of these players is the only one to wear the "C"?

a. Phil Esposito

b. Wayne Cashman

c. Cam Neely

d. Adam Oates

11. Don McKenney recorded the lowest plus/minus season for any Boston captain in 1961-62. How low did he finish?

a. -6

b. -28

c. -31

d. -40

12. In their entire history, the Boston Bruins have never named a goaltender captain of the team.

a. True

b. False

13. In 1967, the Bruins went without a captain for the first time. Which of the following players was NOT chosen as one of their three assistant captains?

    a. Johnny Bucyk
    b. Phil Esposito
    c. Ted Green
    d. Leo Boivin

14. The great Bobby Orr was never a captain for the Bruins teams. How many seasons did he serve as an assistant captain?

    a. 0
    b. 1
    c. 5
    d. 10

15. Which captain holds the record for most points in a season while leading the Bruins, with 101?

    a. Joe Thornton
    b. Fern Flaman
    c. Ray Bourque
    d. Johnny Bucyk

16. The Bruins have never named a Russian player even as an assistant captain, let alone a captain.

    a. True
    b. False

17. Which player was the oldest to wear the "C" for the Boston Bruins, at 42 years old?

a. Terry O'Reilly

b. Ray Bourque

c. Wayne Cashman

d. Zdeno Chara

18. How many Norris Trophies did Ray Bourque win while he was captain of the Bruins?

a. 0

b. 2

c. 5

d. 7

19. Which Bruins captain was once offered a tryout with Major League Baseball's St. Louis Cardinals?

a. Ray Bourque

b. Milt Schmidt

c. Ed Sandford

d. Lionel Hitchman

20. Eddie Shore, the Bruins defenseman considered the NHL's first superstar, declined to become the team's captain because he believed referees were against him and would rule against the Bruins anytime he tried to discuss a penalty with them.

a. True

b. False

QUIZ ANSWERS

1. C – Sprague Cleghorn

2. A – True

3. D – 8

4. B – Ray Bourque

5. B – Lionel Hitchman

6. C – Terry O'Reilly

7. B – False

8. D – 2006

9. D – Joe Thornton

10. B – Wayne Cashman

11. C – -31

12. A – True

13. D – Leo Boivin

14. B – 1

15. A – Joe Thornton

16. A – True

17. D – Zdeno Chara

18. C – 5

19. B – Milt Schmidt

20. B – False

DID YOU KNOW?

1. The longest stretch the Bruins went without an official captain lasted from 1967 until 1972. Johnny Bucyk was the captain in the years prior and following (1966 and 1973).

2. Although 19 men have captained the Bruins throughout their history, only 7 of those players have had their numbers retired by the team.

3. Four Bruins captains recorded no goals during a single season. Fern Flaman went back-to-back seasons without a tally, from 1957-1959.

4. For three seasons, from 1985-1988, the Bruins named Rick Middleton and Ray Bourque co-captains of the team. For the first half of the season, one wore the "C" at home, and the other sported it on the road. Then in the latter half of the season, the arrangement was reversed.

5. Cooney Weiland held the Bruins' captaincy for just one year, when line mate Dit Clapper ceded it to him in 1938-39. The Bruins won the Stanley Cup that year, and Weiland returned the "C" to Clapper for the following season.

6. Despite being brand new to the organization after signing as a free agent in 2006, defenseman Zdeno Chara immediately stepped into the captain's role. They did not regret the choice, as Chara held on to this role for over a decade.

7. The Bruins went without a captain in 2001, after 2000 captain Jason Allison held out in a contract dispute. Allison was eventually traded to the Los Angeles Kings, and the Bruins waited until the following year to replace him as captain.

8. George Owen served the shortest term as Bruins captain, wearing the "C" for just 42 games during the 1931-32 season.

9. Dit Clapper was a busy man in his 40s, as he not only remained captain of the Bruins but also took on the coaching duties for the team.

10. Only Canadians and one Slovakian (Zdeno Chara) have served as captain of the Bruins. Two other countries (America and the Czech Republic) are also represented when considering assistant captains.

CHAPTER 6:

STATISTICALLY SPEAKING

QUIZ TIME!

1. Who is the Bruins all-time leader in goals scored, with 545?

    a. Bobby Orr

    b. Phil Esposito

    c. Johnny Bucyk

    d. Patrice Bergeron

2. In 1963-64, goaltender Eddie Johnston could have used some help. He faced more shots and lost more games than any Boston goalie before or since.

    a. True

    b. False

3. Who is the Bruins' single season leader in goals scored, with 76?

    a. Joe Thornton

    b. Phil Esposito

    c. Johnny Bucyk

    d. Patrice Bergeron

4. This Bruin really picked his spots, showing his accuracy with the highest career shooting percentage for the team.

    a. Dmitri Khristich
    b. Ray Bourque
    c. Charlie Simmer
    d. Stan Jonathan

5. Which player made the biggest difference by being on the ice for Boston, with a career plus/minus of +574?

    a. Ray Bourque
    b. Dallas Smith
    c. Zdeno Chara
    d. Bobby Orr

6. On the Bruins' top 10 list for points scored by a player in a season, how many times does Phil Esposito's name appear?

    a. 5
    b. 6
    c. 8
    d. 9

7. Four Bruins mainstay defensemen (Bobby Orr, Brad Park, Ray Bourque, and Zdeno Chara) all posted the exact same plus/minus (+14) in their first seasons with the club.

    a. True
    b. False

8. Of the four goalies that have recorded over 200 career wins for the Bruins, who has recorded the most?

a. Gerry Cheevers

b. Tiny Thompson

c. Tuukka Rask

d. Frank Brimsek

9. Who holds the single season Bruins record for points per game, at 1.97?

a. Phil Esposito

b. Bill Cowley

c. Bobby Orr

d. Adam Oates

10. Which Bruins goalie set the team record for most wins in a single season, with 40?

a. Tiny Thompson

b. Frank Brimsek

c. Byron Dafoe

d. Pete Peeters

11. This Bruin winger has scored more short-handed goals for the team than anyone else.

a. Brad Marchand

b. Terry O'Reilly

c. P.J. Axelsson

d. Ken Hodge

12. Boston's record for short-handed goals in a season stood for 45 years, before Brian Rolston set the new mark with 9 in 2001-02.

a. True

b. False

13. Among many tough players, who was the only Bruin to reach 300 penalty minutes in a season?

    a. Lyndon Byers
    b. Chris Nilan
    c. Jay Miller
    d. Terry O'Reilly

14. This Bruin laps the competition for most shots taken in a career, firing away over 2,500 times *more often* than the team's second place skater.

    a. Patrice Bergeron
    b. Johnny Bucyk
    c. Rick Middleton
    d. Ray Bourque

15. Bobby Orr had many fine seasons leading the Bruins' defense. Which was the only season where he broke 100 assists for the year?

    a. 1969-70
    b. 1970-71
    c. 1971-72
    d. 1972-73

16. The only Bruin to ever score 50 even-strength goals in a season is Phil Esposito.

    a. True
    b. False

17. Which Bruins goaltender has recorded the most career shutouts for the team, with 74?

a. Tuukka Rask

b. Tiny Thompson

c. Andy Moog

d. Gerry Cheevers

18. Which two teammates posted the highest combined points total in a season for the Bruins?

a. Adam Oates and Cam Neely

b. Patrice Bergeron and David Pastrnak

c. Bobby Orr and Phil Esposito

d. Dit Clapper and Cooney Weiland

19. Nobody comes close to which feisty Bruin, who recorded over 2,000 penalty minutes with the team—almost 500 minutes more than his closest competitor?

a. Terry O'Reilly

b. Eddie Shore

c. Zdeno Chara

d. Mike Milbury

20. Tuukka Rask owns five of the top ten seasons on the Bruins' list of highest save percentages.

a. True

b. False

QUIZ ANSWERS

1. C – Johnny Bucyk

2. A – True

3. B – Phil Esposito

4. C – Charlie Simmer

5. D – Bobby Orr

6. B – 6

7. B – False

8. C – Tuukka Rask

9. B – Bill Cowley

10. D – Pete Peeters

11. A – Brad Marchand

12. A – True

13. C – Jay Miller

14. D – Ray Bourque

15. B – 1970-71

16. A – True

17. B – Tiny Thompson

18. C – Bobby Orr and Phil Esposito

19. A – Terry O'Reilly

20. A – True

DID YOU KNOW?

1. Phil Esposito had to make some extra room in his closet, because he recorded 26 hat tricks (scoring three goals in the same game) during his career. No other Bruin has more than 14.

2. Seventy games played in one year is a lot of work for any goaltender. Jack Gelineau did it in 1950-51 to set the Boston record. Not to be outdone, Jim Henry played 70 games each of the next three seasons to tie the mark.

3. No Bruin has averaged an assist per game over the course of his career; however, Bobby Orr and Adam Oates were close. Orr averaged 0.99 assists per game, and Oates averaged 0.97.

4. So far, five Bruins have managed to crack the magical 50-goal mark in a season. Ken Hodge, Cam Neely, Rick Middleton, and Johnny Bucyk have all done it. Phil Esposito did it five times.

5. If you passed the puck to Phil Esposito in 1970-71, you probably weren't getting it back. Esposito's 550 shots that year are a franchise record that stands over 120 shots higher than second place...which was Esposito again the following year!

6. It is no coincidence that the Bruins' career leader in points, Ray Bourque, is also their career leader in games played. Bourque recorded 1,506 points in 1,518 games.

7. When Cam Neely stepped on the ice in 1993-94, opposing goalies could forget their dreams of a shutout. Neely scored 1.02 goals per game that year: tops in Bruins history.

8. When it really mattered, Johnny Bucyk was "clutch" for the Bruins. He leads the franchise with 88 game-winning goals scored over his storied career.

9. No Bruins goaltender has seen more rubber than Tuukka Rask, who is closing in on 15,000 shots faced during his Boston career.

10. It was a different era. In 1927-28, Bruins goaltender Hal Winkler set a franchise mark that still stands, with 15 shutouts in the season. Oddly, Boston sent him to the minors afterward, and he would never play another NHL game again.

CHAPTER 7:

THE TRADE MARKET

QUIZ TIME!

1. In separate deals in the mid-1920s, the Bruins acquired two players who would go on to captain the team. Who were those players?

    a. Eddie Shore and Lionel Hitchman
    b. Bobby Bauer and Eddie Shore
    c. Lionel Hitchman and Sprague Cleghorn
    d. Sprague Cleghorn and Eddie Shore

2. When the Bruins traded defenseman Ray Bourque so that he could chase an elusive Stanley Cup victory at the end of his career, there were *two* Hall of Famers involved in the deal.

    a. True
    b. False

3. From which team did the Bruins acquire the draft pick used to select franchise cornerstone Ray Bourque?

    a. New York Islanders
    b. Buffalo Sabres

    c. Philadelphia Flyers

    d. Los Angeles Kings

4. In 2005, the Bruins traded captain (and former 1st overall pick) Joe Thornton to the San Jose Sharks. Which pieces did they receive in return?

    a. 3 centers

    b. 1 center, 1 winger, and 1 defenseman

    c. 2 defensemen and 1 winger

    d. 1 goalie, 1 defenseman, and 1 center

5. What did the Bruins receive in trade from the Chicago Blackhawks for goaltender Frank Brimsek?

    a. Glenn Hall

    b. Cash

    c. Future considerations

    d. Free rent of a practice arena

6. When the Bruins acquired Phil Esposito from the Chicago Blackhawks in 1967, they gave up three players in the deal. Which one of the following was NOT included?

    a. Gilles Marotte

    b. Jack Norris

    c. Pit Martin

    d. Fred Stanfield

7. The Bruins have given their players more contracts with no-trade clauses than any other NHL franchise.

    a. True

    b. False

8. One of the Bruins' best trades saw them acquire both Cam Neely and Glen Wesley in exchange for Barry Pederson. Which team regretted making that deal with Boston?

    a. Pittsburgh Penguins
    b. New Jersey Devils
    c. Vancouver Canucks
    d. Hartford Whalers

9. In what year did the Bruins first make a trade for "future considerations"?

    a. 1933
    b. 1955
    c. 1977
    d. 1999

10. At the 2007 NHL trade deadline, the Bruins made three trades involving conditional draft picks. Which of the following was NOT a real condition in one of those trades?

    a. Whether the player re-signed with his new team
    b. Whether the player played more than 80 games before the end of the next season
    c. Whether the player averaged more than 20 minutes per game during the next season
    d. Whether the player scored more than 30 goals during the next season

11. From which team did Boston acquire future Hall-of-Famer Cooney Weiland?

    a. Montreal Canadiens
    b. Detroit Red Wings

c. Chicago Blackhawks

d. New York Rangers

12. In 1982, Boston acquired two players from the Minnesota North Stars. They did not send anyone in return; in exchange, they agreed not to select Brian Bellows in the NHL Draft.

a. True

b. False

13. Who did the Boston Bruins select with the first draft pick acquired by the team, 4th overall, in 1970?

a. Don Tannahill

b. Andre Savard

c. Rick MacLeish

d. Reggie Leach

14. How many draft picks did the Bruins trade to the St. Louis Blues, all for cash, in 1978?

a. 1

b. 2

c. 3

d. 4

15. When franchise icon Eddie Shore came out of retirement, he played just four games for Boston before being traded to which squad?

a. New York Americans

b. Toronto St. Patricks

c. Montreal Canadiens

d. Detroit Red Wings

16. In 1957, the Bruins swapped one future Hall-of-Famer for another, dealing Terry Sawchuk to Detroit for Johnny Bucyk.

    a. True
    b. False

17. To which team did the Bruins deal beloved forward Derek Sanderson?

    a. California Golden Seals
    b. Toronto Maple Leafs
    c. New York Rangers
    d. Vancouver Canucks

18. Who did the Bruins send to the St. Louis Blues in the first trade in which they acquired three types of assets (a player, a draft pick, and cash)?

    a. Johnny McKenzie
    b. Don Awrey
    c. Gilles Gilbert
    d. Mark Howe

19. The largest trade Boston has completed was a 1955 deal involving Terry Sawchuk. How many total players were involved?

    a. 6
    b. 7
    c. 8
    d. 9

20. Boston has made more trades than any other franchise in NHL history.

    a. True
    b. False

QUIZ ANSWERS

1. C – Lionel Hitchman and Sprague Cleghorn

2. A – True

3. D – Los Angeles Kings

4. B – 1 center, 1 winger, and 1 defenseman

5. B – Cash

6. D – Fred Stanfield

7. B – False

8. C – Vancouver Canucks

9. A – 1933

10. D – Whether the player scored more than 30 goals during the next season

11. B – Detroit Red Wings

12. A – True

13. C – Rick MacLeish

14. D – 4

15. A – New York Americans

16. A – True

17. C – New York Rangers

18. B – Don Awrey

19. D – 9

20. B – False

DID YOU KNOW?

1. The very first trade in Bruins history happened on December 8, 1924, when the Bruins acquired Ernie Parkes from the Toronto St. Patricks for cash. Parkes lasted 11 days with Boston before being sent to the Montreal Maroons for George Carroll.

2. Boston has completed a trade with every current NHL franchise except for two: the Nashville Predators and Las Vegas Golden Knights.

3. In one of the biggest trades in their history, the Bruins sent franchise icon Phil Esposito and Carol Vadnais to the New York Rangers for Brad Park, Jean Ratelle, and Joe Zanussi on November 7, 1975. None of these players would win a Stanley Cup with their new franchise.

4. In one of the smallest trades in their history, the Boston Bruins and Colorado Avalanche swapped the last two picks of the 1997 NHL Draft. Colorado got defenseman Steve Lafleur 245th overall, and Boston selected left winger Jay Henderson 246th overall.

5. In 1997, the Bruins traded forward Jozef Stumpel...to the Los Angeles Kings. In 2001, the Bruins acquired Jozef Stumpel...from the Los Angeles Kings. And in 2003, the Bruins again traded Jozef Stumpel...to the Los Angeles Kings.

6. During the 1930s, Boston management often made trades

which included the loan of a player for the remainder of a season. These players were like mercenaries, plying their services elsewhere, and then returning to their original squads when the year ended.

7. Star winger Phil Kessel was traded to the Toronto Maple Leafs in 2009. The Bruins received draft picks they used on eventual stars Tyler Seguin and Dougie Hamilton, but both Seguin and Hamilton were traded away early in their careers.

8. When trading future draft picks was legalized in the NHL, Boston loathed giving them up. The Bruins acquired six picks in five years, before finally giving up one of theirs (a 7th round pick to the Toronto Maple Leafs in 1971).

9. The first time the Bruins were involved in a trade for the top overall pick in the NHL Draft, they acquired it from Colorado in 1981. The Bruins used it to select Gord Kluzak, whose promising career was derailed by injuries.

10. The most lopsided trade, size-wise, in Bruins history, happened in 2018 when the Bruins gave up Ryan Spooner, Matt Belesky, Ryan Lindgren, and 1st and 7th round draft picks, all for New York Ranger winger Rick Nash.

CHAPTER 8:

DRAFT DAY

QUIZ TIME!

1. Who was the first ever player selected by the Bruins in the NHL Entry Draft?

    a. Bobby Orr

    b. Don McKenney

    c. Orest Romashyma

    d. Leo Labine

2. In the 1980s, the Bruins drafted two American players with the last name Sweeney, but the two were not related.

    a. True

    b. False

3. Which player did the Bruins select the first time they had the top overall pick in the NHL Draft?

    a. Alec Campbell

    b. Terry O'Reilly

    c. Joe Bailey

    d. Barry Gibbs

4. In 1987, the Bruins made the most draft selections in franchise history. How many players did they select?

    a. 8
    b. 10
    c. 13
    d. 15

5. The Bruins once drafted the son of which legendary NHL player?

    a. Gordie Howe
    b. Maurice Richard
    c. Wayne Gretzky
    d. Marcel Dionne

6. In 1994, Boston used its first selection on Russian goalie Evgeni Ryabchikov, who failed to play a game in the NHL. This ended an impressive streak of how many years in which Boston's first player selected made it to the NHL?

    a. 14
    b. 19
    c. 25
    d. 28

7. Malfunctioning technology led to a situation in the 2004 Entry Draft where Boston did not get its 5th round pick in on time and had to wait until another team picked before they could select their choice.

    a. True
    b. False

8. Fan favorite Terry O'Reilly was selected in the 1ˢᵗ round by the Boston Bruins in 1971. Which junior league did he play in?

   a. WHL
   b. ICAU
   c. OHL
   d. QMJHL

9. Which brother of a Bruins icon was drafted by Boston, but never played in the NHL?

   a. Richard Bourque
   b. Jim Cashman
   c. Alex Esposito
   d. Mike Sweeney

10. What was the main reason 1ˢᵗ overall pick Gord Kluzak played less than 300 games as a defenseman for Boston?

   a. Decided to become a broadcaster
   b. Traded to Toronto Maple Leafs
   c. Suffered a major concussion
   d. Suffered a major knee injury

11. Boston first selected Europeans (including one Finn and one Swede) in the Entry Draft in which year?

   a. 1970
   b. 1975
   c. 1980
   d. 1985

12. Boston selected Rob Cheevers, son of franchise star Gerry Cheevers, in the 7th round of the 1987 NHL Draft.

    a. True
    b. False

13. The Bruins struck gold in the 1997 NHL Draft, selecting Joe Thornton with the 1st overall pick, along with fellow star Sergei Samsonov, who was selected with which number pick?

    a. 3rd
    b. 8th
    c. 21st
    d. 144th

14. In the 9th round of the NHL Draft, in 1978, Boston would select which player, who would go on to become the last NHL player to play in the league without a helmet?

    a. Ron Duguay
    b. Al Iafrate
    c. Randy Carlyle
    d. Craig McTavish

15. What is the highest round of the draft in which the Bruins ever selected a goaltender?

    a. 1st round
    b. 2nd round
    c. 3rd round
    d. 4th round

16. In 2015, the Bruins had three 1st round selections, back to back to back.

    a. True

    b. False

17. The Bruins struck out mightily in the 2007 NHL Draft, selecting six skaters who scored a total of how many NHL goals?

    a. 0

    b. 2

    c. 6

    d. 24

18. In 1979, the Bruins selected franchise icon Ray Bourque with the 8th overall pick. How many other defensemen were chosen ahead of him?

    a. 0

    b. 1

    c. 3

    d. 5

19. Current franchise cornerstones Patrice Bergeron and David Krejci were selected in which round in back-to-back years?

    a. 1st round

    b. 2nd round

    c. 4th round

    d. 7th round

20. Star defenseman P.K. Subban was taken by the Bruins in the 1st round but had grown up as such a Canadiens fan that he held out until he was traded to Montreal.

    a. True
    b. False

QUIZ ANSWERS

1. C – Orest Romashyma

2. A – True

3. D – Barry Gibbs

4. C – 13

5. A – Gordie Howe

6. B – 19

7. B – False

8. C – OHL

9. A – Richard Bourque

10. D – Suffered a major knee injury

11. B – 1975

12. A – True

13. B – 8th

14. D – Craig McTavish

15. A – 1st round

16. A – True

17. A – 0

18. C – 3

19. B – 2nd round

20. B – False

DID YOU KNOW?

1. In the inaugural NHL Entry Draft of 1963, the Bruins selected four players, none of whom ever skated in an NHL game.

2. When the Iron Curtain fell, the Bruins jumped into the newfound player pool quickly, selecting 3 Russians, 2 Latvians, 1 German, 1 Pole, 1 Slovak, and 1 Czech in the 1991-92 Drafts.

3. During the 1st round of the 2007 NHL Draft, Boston passed on Angelo Esposito (son of franchise icon Phil) to select a center named Zach Hamill. They regretted passing on Max Pacioretty more, though. Pacioretty has gone on to score over 280 goals in the NHL, while neither Hamill nor Esposito ever recorded a goal.

4. In 1964, the Bruins drafted future Hall of Fame goalie Ken Dryden in the 3rd round. Within days, he was traded to the Montreal Canadiens. Dryden himself did not realize until the middle of the next decade that he had originally been drafted by Boston.

5. Boston was in line for the top two overall picks in the 1970 Amateur Draft. However, due to expansion, the Buffalo Sabres selected Hall-of-Famer Gilbert Perreault 1st overall, depriving the Bruins of a potential franchise player.

6. In 1966, the Bruins chose Barry Gibbs with the 1st overall pick, passing on defenseman Brad Park, who went 2nd to

the New York Rangers. Years later, Boston would remedy this mistake by trading for Park, who went on to play eight seasons with the team.

7. The first Bruins draft pick who went on to play 1,000 NHL games was center Ivan Boldirev. Only thirteen of those games were with Boston, as he bounced between six NHL teams during his long career.

8. The 2006 NHL Draft was an excellent one for the Bruins, as they chose three wingers who would all go on to stardom: Phil Kessel, Milan Lucic, and Brad Marchand.

9. In 1984, the Bruins spent an 8th round pick on defenseman Don Sweeney. The pick paid off in multiple ways, as Sweeney played over 1,000 NHL games and, in retirement, made draft picks himself after becoming the Bruins' general manager.

10. The 2010 draft narrative centered around "Taylor vs. Tyler," as Taylor Hall and Tyler Seguin vied to be chosen 1st overall. Hall went first, and Boston, with the 2nd pick, was left to select Seguin, who became an excellent player in the league…although the Bruins traded him to Dallas.

CHAPTER 9:

GOALTENDER TIDBITS

QUIZ TIME!

1. How did star goalie Cecil Thompson get the nickname "Tiny"?

   a. Opposing skaters said that he only allowed them tiny openings to shoot at.
   b. He weighed only 130 pounds as a rookie.
   c. His goals against average was always extremely low.
   d. He was the tallest player on his team as a teenager.

2. Boston's Bill Ranford was dealt to Edmonton for Andy Moog, traded back to the Bruins, and then shipped to Washington for another goalie, Jim Carey.

   a. True
   b. False

3. What was unique about Gerry Cheevers's goalie mask?

   a. It was used as a model for horror film villain Jason Voorhees's mask.
   b. It rotated between three versions of solid colors: white for home, black for the road, and gold for the playoffs.

c. It was painted with a line of fake stitches in every spot where a puck hit it.

d. It was made of thin steel, which gave off a metallic "clang" when it was struck during games.

4. Workhorse Bruins goalie "Sugar" Jim Henry led the NHL in minutes played for how many seasons while playing for Boston?

   a. 4
   b. 3
   c. 6
   d. 10

5. Bruins netminder Tuukka Rask's wife gave birth to a daughter during which round of the 2014 Stanley Cup playoffs (but never missed a game)?

   a. 1st round
   b. 2nd round
   c. Semifinals
   d. Finals

6. Which Boston goalie declined to join the team on the customary championship trip to the White House, because he disagreed with the politics of the president at the time?

   a. Eddie Johnston
   b. Tim Thomas
   c. Tiny Thompson
   d. Tuukka Rask

7. In his first start after signing with the Bruins to back up Tuukka Rask, Jaroslav Halak posted a 4-0 shutout over the Buffalo Sabres.

    a. True
    b. False

8. Hall-of-Famer Bernie Parent began his career with the Boston Bruins. How was he obtained by the Philadelphia Flyers?

    a. Signed as a free agent
    b. Included in a trade
    c. Selected in an expansion draft
    d. Returned to them out of retirement

9. Which Bruins goalie was dubbed "The Canadian Tretiak" by a teammate, in a nod to Russia's legendary national team goaltender?

    a. Andy Moog
    b. Tim Thomas
    c. Bill Ranford
    d. Reggie Lemelin

10. Manny Fernandez played just 28 games between the pipes for the Bruins in 2008-09, but managed to win which award?

    a. Vezina Trophy
    b. William M. Jennings Trophy
    c. Bill Masterson Memorial Trophy
    d. Calder Trophy

11. Which Bruins goalie is the only netminder in NHL history to be nominated for the Vezina Trophy in both of his first two seasons?

    a. Byron Dafoe
    b. Tuukka Rask
    c. Gerry Cheevers
    d. Jim Carey

12. Bruins goalie Harry Lumley made his NHL debut at just 17 years old; the youngest goaltender to ever play in the NHL.

    a. True
    b. False

13. What was Andrew Raycroft's goals against average during his Calder Trophy winning rookie season in 2003-04?

    a. 1.93
    b. 2.05
    c. 2.18
    d. 2.20

14. Which of the following is NOT one of Bruins goalie Anton Khudobin's favorite pastimes away from the ice?

    a. Playing Ping-Pong
    b. Watching Jason Statham movies
    c. Building treehouses
    d. Building Legos

15. Who was the only NHL goaltender to reach 300 wins faster than former Bruin great, Andy Moog?

a. Jacques Plante

b. Terry Sawchuk

c. Grant Fuhr

d. Ken Dryden

16. Due to a rugby injury, goalie Terry Sawchuk's right arm was shorter than his left one.

a. True

b. False

17. Although Montreal defeated the Bruins in seven games in the 1979 playoffs, the Habs' Steve Shutt said, "Gilles Gilbert stood on his head. He was the reason they got to the seventh game." In how many of those games was Gilbert named the first star?

a. 0

b. 1

c. 2

d. 3

18. Jacques Plante was the first goaltender in the NHL to introduce a face mask. Which Boston Bruin was the second to ever wear one?

a. Harry Lumley

b. Frank Brimsek

c. Don Simmons

d. Terry Sawchuk

19. Bruins goalie Marco Baron left the team, and the country, after his career ended. To which country did he emigrate?

a. Thailand

b. Jamaica

c. Monaco

d. Switzerland

20. After his NHL career ended, Bruins goalie John Grahame wanted to keep playing, so he joined a start-up hockey league in Japan.

a. True

b. False

QUIZ ANSWERS

1. D – He was the tallest player on his team as a teenager.
2. A – True
3. C – It was painted with a line of fake stitches in every spot where a puck hit it.
4. B – 3
5. A – 1st round
6. B – Tim Thomas
7. A – True
8. C – Selected in an expansion draft
9. D – Reggie Lemelin
10. B – William M. Jennings Trophy
11. D – Jim Carey
12. A – True
13. B – 2.05
14. C – Building treehouses
15. A – Jacques Plante
16. A – True
17. D – 3
18. C – Don Simmons
19. D – Switzerland
20. B – False

DID YOU KNOW?

1. The Bruins briefly employed a national hero as their goaltender, Jim Craig, who led the United States to an upset gold medal victory over the Soviet Union at the 1980 Olympics in Lake Placid, played 23 games for Boston in 1981.

2. Former Bruins goaltender Byron Dafoe started a business called Diamante Custom Automation after his retirement. He uses his B.C. mansion as a showpiece to demonstrate to potential clients how the remote-control heating, lighting, theatre, and other features work.

3. Boston goalie Andy Moog has the second highest winning percentage of any retired netminder who has not been elected to the Hall of Fame.

4. In 1984, Pete Peeters was ejected from a game against the Hartford Whalers. Oddly, he was serving as Boston's backup goalie that night, and was ejected while sitting on the bench.

5. Seven goalies who have played for the Bruins have been enshrined in the Hall of Fame. The most recent was Gerry Cheevers, who was elected in 1985.

6. Pioneering goalie Jacques Plante made a cameo appearance of 10 games for the Bruins in his final NHL season. He earned a shutout in his Boston debut.

7. The Bruins swapped rookie of the year goalie Andrew Raycroft to the Toronto Maple Leafs for even younger goalie Tuukka Rask. Rask has gone on to have a much longer career, playing in two All-Star Games and winning the Vezina Trophy in 2014.

8. Jerry Toppazzini is in the Bruins record book with the most goals scored by a goalie, with 15. Normally a forward, Toppazzini qualified for the record when he went between the pipes for 30 seconds at the end of a game in which starter Don Simmons was injured. He did not face a single shot.

9. Bruins great Eddie Johnston, who backstopped the team to Stanley Cup victories in the 1970s, went on to become general manager of the Pittsburgh Penguins, and was the man who drafted superstar Mario Lemieux.

10. Hall-of-Famer Gerry Cheevers, a legendary Bruins goaltender, had a chance to own even more space in the Bruins record book. Cheevers spent four years playing in the upstart WHA for the Cleveland Crusaders, making All-Star Games there before returning to Boston.

CHAPTER 10:

ODDS & ENDS

QUIZ TIME!

1. What is the current Boston Bruins goal song called?

    a. "Blow the Lid Off"

    b. "Shipping Up to Boston"

    c. "KernKraft 400"

    d. "Too Strong"

2. The Bruins have faced every other Original Six team in the Stanley Cup Finals at least once in their history.

    a. True

    b. False

3. Which St. Louis Blues goalie sags backwards into his net in the famous photo of Bobby Orr flying through the air after scoring an overtime goal in the 1970 Stanley Cup Finals?

    a. Jacques Plante

    b. Ken Sabourin

    c. Chico Resch

    d. Glenn Hall

4. Longtime Bruins captain Zdeno Chara was signed to a 5-year contract as a free agent in 2006. How much money did the Bruins pay him to leave the Ottawa Senators?

    a. $18 million
    b. $24.5 million
    c. $29 million
    d. $37.5 million

5. Facing the Florida Panthers, how long did it take Bruins winger Mike Knuble to set the NHL record for fastest two goals in a game?

    a. 14 seconds
    b. 27 seconds
    c. 51 seconds
    d. 1 minute, 6 seconds

6. Which future stud was signed as a free agent by Boston in 2008, and then dealt to Atlanta for Rich Peverley?

    a. Phil Kessel
    b. Joe Thornton
    c. Blake Wheeler
    d. Milan Lucic

7. When the NHL first split its teams into divisions, there were only two, and Boston was placed in the American Division.

    a. True
    b. False

8. Two Bruins have achieved the 50-goal plateau in three or more seasons. Which Bruins were they?

   a. Ken Hodge and Johnny Bucyk

   b. Phil Esposito and Cam Neely

   c. Johnny Bucyk and Rick Middleton

   d. Dit Clapper and Phil Esposito

9. With expansion in 1967, the NHL changed its divisional structure. Where were the Bruins placed?

   a. American Northeast Division

   b. Norris Division

   c. Original Six Division

   d. East Division

10. Revered Bruins forward Ken Hodge was born in which country?

   a. United States

   b. Canada

   c. England

   d. Bahamas

11. On December 23, 1979, a brawl broke out at a Bruins/Rangers game. When a fan tried to steal a Bruins stick, forward Mike Milbury began to pummel the fan with what item?

   a. The stick being stolen

   b. The fan's own shoe

   c. A full water bottle

   d. The fan's wife's purse

12. The Bruins were the very first NHL franchise to ever use a Zamboni machine to resurface the ice between periods.

   a. True
   b. False

13. Three times, Boston has recorded its franchise record for largest margin of victory over an opponent. How many goals make up this margin of victory?

   a. 5
   b. 6
   c. 9
   d. 11

14. The Bruins won five Stanley Cup championships during the twentieth century. How many times did they lose in the Finals?

   a. 6
   b. 9
   c. 12
   d. 15

15. In 1974, the NHL's newly designed two-conference structure placed the Bruins into a division named for which honored namesake?

   a. Patrick Division
   b. Norris Division
   c. Adams Division
   d. Smythe Division

16. Current Bruins owner Jeremy Jacobs has owned the franchise for a record 45 years.

    a. True
    b. False

17. For 23 years, between 1959-1982, the Bruins played dozens of times in Montreal without doing what?

    a. Scoring a hat trick
    b. Recording a shutout
    c. Playing an entire game without any fights
    d. Ending the game in a tie

18. In which city does the Bruins' AHL affiliate team play?

    a. Worcester, Massachusetts
    b. Providence, Rhode Island
    c. Hartford, Connecticut
    d. Concord, New Hampshire

19. The high-flying Bruins of 1970-71 placed how many skaters among the league's top 10 scorers?

    a. 4
    b. 5
    c. 6
    d. 7

20. In a poll during their 75th season of existence, Bruins fans voted Eddie Shore as the greatest Bruin of all time.

    a. True
    b. False

QUIZ ANSWERS

1. C – "KernKraft 400"

2. A – True

3. D – Glenn Hall

4. D – $37.5 million

5. B – 27 seconds

6. C – Blake Wheeler

7. A – True

8. B – Phil Esposito and Cam Neely

9. D – East Division

10. C – England

11. B – The fan's own shoe

12. A – True

13. D – 11

14. C – 12

15. C – Adams Division

16. A – True

17. A – Scoring a hat trick

18. B – Providence, Rhode Island

19. D – 7

20. B – False

DID YOU KNOW?

1. Bruins player Billy Coutu was the first to ever receive a lifelong suspension from the NHL. He assaulted a referee after losing a playoff game in 1927 to earn the ban.

2. The 2008-09 Bruins went 4-0 against the Carolina Hurricanes in the regular season and finished as Eastern Conference champions with 116 points. Unfortunately, in the playoffs, they faced the Hurricanes again and lost the series 4-3.

3. In 1981, Peter McNab became the first Bruin to attempt a penalty shot during the Stanley Cup playoffs. He did not score.

4. The NHL's YoungStars game ignited excitement among Boston fans in 2007, when young Bruin Phil Kessel scored a hat trick just a month after completing successful cancer treatments.

5. In 1958, the Bruins iced a player named Willie O'Ree, who became the first to break the NHL's color barrier. Despite a major eye injury, the talented O'Ree had a long hockey career, but only skated in 45 games for Boston.

6. Bruins defenseman Bobby Orr is the only player in NHL history to win the Conn Smythe, James Norris, Art Ross, and Hart Memorial Trophies in a single season. He also led the Bruins to a Stanley Cup that year.

7. For the 2013 season, the NHL realigned according to the geographical positioning of its teams. Two conferences with four divisions were created. Boston was placed in the Eastern Conference's Atlantic Division, where they have remained ever since.

8. During the 1988 Stanley Cup Final against the Edmonton Oilers, Game 4 was suspended after the lights in Boston Garden went out. The series resumed two days later in Edmonton, but the change of venue hardly mattered. The Oilers won in a four-game sweep.

9. Bruins owner Jeremy Jacobs partners with John Henry, the owner of the Boston Red Sox, in owning the New England Sports Network, which broadcasts much content for both teams.

10. In 2000, Marty McSorley angrily swung his stick at Donald Brashear's head. He was fined $72,000 and suspended for 23 games, but neither the Bruins nor any other team would put him back on the ice afterward, and McSorley never played again.

CHAPTER 11:

BRUINS ON THE BLUE LINE

QUIZ TIME!

1. Leo Boivin was captain of the Bruins for how many of his 12 years with the club?

   a. 0
   b. 4
   c. 8
   d. 12

2. After Boston's Mike Milbury brawled with fans in Madison Square Garden in 1979, the NHL responded by mandating higher glass separating players and the crowd in all arenas.

   a. True
   b. False

3. Before being drafted 1st overall by the Bruins, defenseman Gord Kluzak represented Canada at the World Junior Championship. After winning gold, he and his teammates sang "O Canada" on the ice. Why?

a. The arena's public address system malfunctioned and could not be heard by the crowd.

b. The team did not approve of the singer hired and wanted to drown her out.

c. Organizers did not think Canada would win and did not have a copy of the anthem.

d. Organizers accidentally played the wrong anthem.

4. Boston captain Lionel Hitchman was not only a hockey player, but also a member of which organization?

a. The Massachusetts Chamber of Commerce

b. The Greater Boston Firefighter's Brigade

c. The Yale Skull and Bones Club

d. The Royal Canadian Mounted Police

5. Which Bruin was the first rookie defenseman in the NHL to score four times in the first five playoff games he appeared in?

a. Torey Krug

b. Bobby Orr

c. Ray Bourque

d. Glen Wesley

6. This Bruins defenseman was compared to Ray Bourque after being drafted one spot lower than Bourque had been and making the NHL All-Rookie Team in his first year.

a. Torey Krug

b. Kyle McLaren

c. Dougie Hamilton

d. Charlie McAvoy

7. Boston defenseman Brad Park's first name is Douglas.

    a. True
    b. False

8. Which of the following facts about Bruins captain Zdeno Chara is NOT true?

    a. He is one of just three European-born NHLers to captain his team to a Stanley Cup victory.
    b. He speaks six languages.
    c. He has a legal real estate license.
    d. He traditionally skydives once every off-season.

9. Although he had a reputation as tough player, Adam McQuaid suffered a concussion in 2010 after doing what?

    a. Slipping in the shower
    b. Tripping over his suitcase
    c. Being head-butted by a dog he was petting
    d. Slapping a mosquito that landed on his temple

10. How old was phenom Bobby Orr when he was signed by the Boston Bruins?

    a. 8
    b. 10
    c. 12
    d. 14

11. Which Bruins defender was the first to lead the league in plus/minus when it started being tracked as a formal statistic?

    a. Ray Bourque

b. Glen Wesley

c. Bobby Orr

d. Dallas Smith

12. Boston defenseman Dennis Seidenberg was the first ever German-born player to win the Stanley Cup.

a. True

b. False

13. Which Providence Bruin won the Eddie Shore Award for best AHL defenseman in 2008-09 before being called up to Boston the following year?

a. Johnny Boychuk

b. Dennis Seidenberg

c. Hal Gill

d. Kyle McLaren

14. Why was Fern Flaman rushed up to the big leagues to join the Bruins at a young age?

a. He broke scoring records for the Bruins' minor league squad.

b. He had already grown larger than several Boston players.

c. The Bruins were suffering from an epidemic of the flu.

d. There was a shortage of players due to World War II.

15. Bruins mainstay Don Sweeney played over 1,000 NHL games with the club. What is his all-time rank for games played for Boston?

a. 9th

b. 7th

c. 4th

d. 1st

16. Boston defenseman Glen Wesley ranks in the NHL's top 40 all-time in games played, on-ice goals for, and on-ice goals against.

    a. True

    b. False

17. Ex Bruins defender Garry Galley was the host of a radio show called what, on TSN Radio, after his retirement?

    a. *More On Sports*

    b. *For the Defense*

    c. *The Hockey Enthusiast*

    d. *Shoot Your Shot*

18. William "Flash" Hollett lived out a dream by scoring a third-period goal for the Bruins in their 1939 Stanley Cup clinching game against his former team. Which team did he send to defeat?

    a. New York Rangers

    b. Detroit Red Wings

    c. Montreal Canadiens

    d. Toronto Maple Leafs

19. Hal Laycoe's NHL career was put on hold during World War II while he served in which branch of the armed forces?

a. Army

b. Air Force

c. Navy

d. Marines

20. Bruins defenseman Eddie Shore was one of the original organizers of the Ice Capades.

a. True

b. False

QUIZ ANSWERS

1. B – 4

2. A – True

3. C – Organizers did not think Canada would win and did not have a copy of the anthem.

4. D – The Royal Canadian Mounted Police

5. A – Torey Krug

6. B – Kyle McLaren

7. A – True

8. D – He traditionally skydives once every off-season.

9. B – Tripping over his suitcase

10. C – 12

11. D – Dallas Smith

12. B – False

13. A – Johnny Boychuk

14. D – There was a shortage of players due to World War II.

15. C – 4th

16. B – False

17. A – *More On Sports*

18. D – Toronto Maple Leafs

19. C – Navy

20. A – True

DID YOU KNOW?

1. The incomparable Bobby Orr remains the only defenseman in NHL history to ever win the Art Ross Trophy for most points in a single season. He did it twice, in 1969-70 and 1974-75.

2. Phil Esposito was not the only Bruin to play in the famous 1972 Summit Series between Canada and Russia. With less fanfare, defenseman Don Awrey and winger Wayne Cashman also appeared in two games in the series.

3. Ray Bourque played more games in the NHL than any other player before finally winning the Stanley Cup. He suited up for 1,826 games, the last of which came when he finally took home the title in 2001.

4. Eddie Shore, famed for his toughness, once had his ear nearly severed in an on-ice incident. He rejected several doctors who recommended amputation, then refused anesthetic from the doctor who finally agreed to re-attach it.

5. Bruins All-Star and Lady Byng Trophy winner Bill Quackenbush was assessed only 95 penalty minutes throughout his 774-game NHL career. Official records are not kept, but his average of 7 seconds of penalty time per game would be among the lowest of all time for any position.

6. In 1969, All-Star defenseman Ted Green was involved in a

stick-swinging incident with opponent Wayne Maki. Green suffered brain damage and a broken skull, and missed the rest of the season including the Bruins' Stanley Cup victory. For the first time in NHL history, both players were charged with assault.

7. At 6 feet 9 inches tall, Bruins defender Zdeno Chara is the tallest player to ever skate in the NHL. He has special permission from the league to use a stick that is longer than the rule book normally permits.

8. Bruins defenseman Nick Boynton has openly struggled with his mental health after many concussions, and became addicted to alcohol, sleeping pills, painkillers, and other drugs. Blaming his enforcer's hockey life, he has been quoted as saying, "They can scratch my name off that cup, if I could make it so that I wouldn't have had to experience all this pain and sorrow."

9. Known more for his size (6 feet 7 inches, 250 pounds) than his skill, Bruins defender Hal Gill once had his picture taken with some large construction pylons. He tweeted it out, along with the caption: "I'm the highest paid one!".

10. Ed Westfall swung between defense and winger for the Boston Bruins, and was often tasked with checking the opposition's top player. He was so effective in this role he earned the nickname "Shadow."

CHAPTER 12:

CENTERS OF ATTENTION

QUIZ TIME!

1. In 1981-82, Barry Pederson established the record for most goals by a Bruins rookie at 44. He finished second in the Calder Trophy voting to which player?

    a. Wayne Gretzky

    b. Peter Stastny

    c. Steve Larmer

    d. Dale Hawerchuk

2. Before Phil Esposito joined the Boston Bruins, he played with his brother Tony for the Chicago Blackhawks.

    a. True

    b. False

3. Which center, known as the "Ultimate Bruin," is the only person to hold the positions of player, captain, general manager, and coach of the franchise?

    a. Milt Schmidt

    b. Art Ross

c. Cooney Weiland

d. Dit Clapper

4. In 2008, David Krejci scored his first NHL goal against the Carolina Hurricanes, but it did not count in the official record books, for what reason?

   a. It was waived off due to a high stick.

   b. It was disallowed because the play was offsides.

   c. It was scored during a tiebreaker shootout.

   d. It was ruled to have been directed in with a distinct kicking motion.

5. This center was the most valuable piece acquired by the Bruins from Colorado in the famous "Ray Bourque trade."

   a. Brian Rolston

   b. Samuel Pahlsson

   c. Dave Andreychuk

   d. Joe Thornton

6. Which center took the first ever penalty shot awarded to the Bruins during the Stanley Cup playoffs, on April 9, 1981?

   a. Tom Fergus

   b. Peter McNab

   c. Barry Pederson

   d. Mike Krushelnyski

7. Boston pivot Bob Sweeney had a sister-in-law who was a flight attendant on one of the planes that crashed into the World Trade Center on September 11, 2001.

a. True

b. False

8. Which Bruin followed Ray Bourque's long reign as Bruins captain, but held the post for only one season?

a. Joe Thornton

b. Patrice Bergeron

c. Joe Juneau

d. Jason Allison

9. Bruins center Patrice Bergeron excels in all situations on the ice. He has been recognized with the Frank Selke Award for best defensive play from a forward four times, tying an NHL record with which player?

a. Sergei Fedorov

b. Bob Gainey

c. Pavel Datsyuk

d. Guy Carbonneau

10. In fourteen NHL seasons, how many times was Fred Stanfield assessed more than 14 penalty minutes in a year?

a. 0

b. 1

c. 7

d. 14

11. Which of the following facts about German-born Bruins center Marco Sturm is NOT true?

a. His nickname with the team is "German."

b. His favorite non-NHL sports team is Bayern Munich.

c. His favorite food is schnitzel.

d. His circle of friends includes David Hasselhoff.

12. In the 1997 Draft, the Bruins took two centers: Joe Thornton 1st overall and Sergei Samsonov 8th overall. Samsonov outperformed Thornton as a rookie and won the Calder Trophy.

a. True

b. False

13. Young and popular with the female crowd, Boston center Tyler Seguin was part of a much publicized "Win a Date with Tyler Seguin" contest through which business?

a. Boston Pizza

b. Dunkin' Donuts

c. Liberty Mutual

d. Red Lobster

14. Bruins center Craig Janney was born near Boston and represented Team USA in which tournament?

a. 1972 Summit Series

b. 1987 Rendez-Vous

c. 1979 Challenge Cup

d. 1988 Winter Olympics

15. Which Lady Byng winning Bruins center was so gentle and kind, teammates claimed "he'd never even destroyed a hockey stick"?

a. Craig Janney

b. Jason Allison

   c. Jean Ratelle

   d. Peter McNab

16. More Bruins centers have won the Art Ross Trophy than centers on any other NHL team.

   a. True

   b. False

17. Two-time NHL MVP Bill Cowley was selected by the Bruins in a dispersal draft after which other team ceased to exist?

   a. California Golden Seals

   b. Cleveland Barons

   c. Ottawa Senators

   d. St. Louis Eagles

18. Jozef Stumpel played professional hockey for an incredible 29 years. During how many of those years did he spend time with the Boston Bruins?

   a. 4

   b. 8

   c. 14

   d. 22

19. Fast-living Bruin Derek Sanderson enjoyed being a celebrity as much as being a Bruin. In 1968, he created a chain of singles bars with this football star.

   a. Joe Namath

   b. Johnny Unitas

   c. Deacon Jones

   d. Dick Butkus

20. Bruins center Gregory Campbell and his friend Peter Frates invented the much publicized "Ice Bucket Challenge" to raise awareness for ALS (Lou Gehrig's disease) among the general public.

    a. True

    b. False

QUIZ ANSWERS

1. D – Dale Hawerchuk

2. B – False

3. A – Milt Schmidt

4. C – It was scored during a tiebreaker shootout.

5. A – Brian Rolston

6. B – Peter McNab

7. A – True

8. D – Jason Allison

9. B – Bob Gainey

10. B – 1

11. D – His circle of friends includes David Hasselhoff.

12. A – True

13. B – Dunkin' Donuts

14. D – 1988 Winter Olympics

15. C – Jean Ratelle

16. B – False

17. D – St. Louis Eagles

18. B – 8

19. A – Joe Namath

20. A –

DID YOU KNOW?

1. Bruins center Andre Savard was well-traveled in his post-playing career. He became assistant coach with the Pittsburgh Penguins, coach with the Quebec Nordiques, scout for the Ottawa Senators, and general manager for the Montreal Canadiens.

2. The Linseman family holds the OHL record for most brothers to play in the league, with John, Mike, Steve, Ted, and Ken all taking the ice. Ken was the only one to graduate to the NHL, where he became a Bruins favorite for several years.

3. Tragically Hip singer (and Boston Bruins fan) Gord Downie wrote a song called "You Me and the B's." In the lyrics, he complains about Boston's ill-fated trade of center Joe Thornton to the San Jose Sharks in 2005.

4. Boston center Marc Savard had bad luck with injuries. He twice suffered concussions after hits by Matt Cooke of the Penguins and Matt Hunwick of the Colorado Avalanche. The latter hit took place in 2011, and Savard dealt with post-concussion symptoms for years. He never played in the NHL again, but did not announce his retirement until 2018.

5. Fleming MacKell showed extreme loyalty to the Bruins franchise he'd spent the 1950s with. In 1960, rather than be traded, he chose to retire as a Bruin, and became a coach in the AHL instead.

6. During his brother Tony's first NHL game as a goalie for the Chicago Blackhawks, Bruins center Phil Esposito scored two goals. Tony got his revenge in their next matchup, posting a shutout. Both games ended in a tie.

7. Don McKenney had his choice of career paths in 1954. He turned down a contract with Major League Baseball's Brooklyn Dodgers to play for the Bruins instead.

8. When Bruins center Steve Kasper eventually moved on to become the team's head coach, his tenure did not go well. It didn't help that he made an enemy of franchise star Cam Neely, by benching him for a full game with zero shifts against the Toronto Maple Leafs.

9. Boston great Cooney Weiland had an excellent sense of timing. He bookended his career with Stanley Cup victories, winning in 1928-29 as a rookie, over the New York Rangers, and again in his final season, 1938-39 over the Toronto Maple Leafs.

10. Bruins center Adam Oates originally dropped out of high school but returned after not being selected in the NHL Entry Draft. He worked with a skating coach, graduated, and then signed the biggest rookie contract in the NHL.

CHAPTER 13:

THE WINGERS TAKE FLIGHT

QUIZ TIME!

1. Leo "The Lion" Labine spent a decade in Boston, most frequently playing with which other winger on his line?

    a. Johnny Bucyk

    b. Real Chevrefils

    c. Harry Oliver

    d. Stan Jonathan

2. Winger Glen Murray had two different stints with the Boston Bruins, separated by almost a decade spent with the Pittsburgh Penguins and Los Angeles Kings.

    a. True

    b. False

3. Which Bruins winger once set up his own brother for a goal against the Hartford Whalers?

    a. Cam Neely

    b. Mike Knuble

    c. Keith Crowder

    d. Randy Burridge

4. Free agent winger Martin Lapointe signed with the Boston Bruins in 2001, but he quickly became seen as the most overpaid player in the league, with a contract worth how much?

   a. $4 million
   b. $8 million
   c. $10 million
   d. $16 million

5. Which of Boston's best defensive forwards scored 21 short-handed goals with the team and mentored Steve Kasper to become the same type of player as he was approaching retirement?

   a. Rick Middleton
   b. Don Marcotte
   c. Brad Marchand
   d. Derek Sanderson

6. Right winger David Pastrnak was an instant success upon arriving in Boston, and at just 21 years old, broke whose record for youngest player to score 6 points in an NHL playoff game?

   a. Bobby Orr
   b. Wayne Gretzky
   c. Mario Lemieux
   d. Teemu Selanne

7. Left winger Vic Stasiuk scored 68 points in 1960, reaching a career high. The following season, he was dealt to the Detroit Red Wings.

a. True

b. False

8. Which pesky Bruins winger has been disciplined by the NHL nine times, including five suspensions and six fines, along with various warnings?

   a. Milan Lucic

   b. Lyndon Byers

   c. Terry O'Reilly

   d. Brad Marchand

9. Tough guy Lyndon Byers became a popular figure in Boston culture. Which of the following did he NOT participate in?

   a. Acting in a recurring role on Boston native Denis Leary's TV show *Rescue Me*

   b. Hosting a Boston area sports talk show on morning radio

   c. Modelling clothing in a series of shows for Boston designer Denise Hajjar

   d. Appearing in a music video by well-known Boston band Extreme

10. In his Bruins career, spanning nine seasons, how many times did right winger Ken Hodge record at least 20 goals in a season?

    a. 3

    b. 6

    c. 8

    d. 9

11. Bruins winger Stan Jonathan worked at which dangerous job as a teenager, before developing into a force as a hockey player?

    a. High-rise building rigger

    b. Salvage diver

    c. Hot air balloon pilot

    d. Coal miner

12. Massachusetts-born winger Steve Heinze requested to wear number 57, thinking it might lead to endorsement opportunities with a famous ketchup company, but was prohibited by his coach.

    a. True

    b. False

13. At 43 years old, Bruins winger Mark Recchi was the oldest player to score a Stanley Cup Finals goal when the Bruins won in 2011. He is the second oldest player ever to win the Cup, behind only who?

    a. Ray Bourque

    b. Chris Chelios

    c. Dave Andreychuk

    d. Gordie Howe

14. Left winger Johnny Bucyk finished his career with the Bruins with the 4th most all-time points in the NHL. Which player was NOT ahead of him?

    a. Stan Mikita

    b. Phil Esposito

c. Maurice Richard

d. Gordie Howe

15. This Bruins winger could score in any situation, but he is also tops in the Boston record book in short-handed goals, with 25.

   a. David Pastrnak

   b. Wayne Cashman

   c. Rick Middleton

   d. John McKenzie

16. Among Randy Burridge's other nicknames ("Animal," "Garbage," "Stump"), he became known for the "Stump Pump," a fist pump he used to celebrate some of his Bruins goals.

   a. True

   b. False

17. Enforcer Terry O'Reilly was mentioned as actor Adam Sandler's favorite hockey player in which hit movie?

   a. *The Water Boy*

   b. *Billy Madison*

   c. *Punch Drunk Love*

   d. *Happy Gilmore*

18. Which Bruins winger was the last player from the Original Six era to hang up his skates in retirement?

   a. Wayne Cashman

   b. Ken Hodge

   c. Harry Oliver

   d. Vic Stasiuk

19. P.J. Axelsson was known for his children's charity work in Boston, including his partnership with Cradles to Crayons and his famous PJ Drive to collect what item for kids in need?

    a. Food
    b. Jackets
    c. Pajamas
    d. Books

20. Bruins winger Bobby Schmautz was famous for aiming high with his shots, and once said, "If it ain't in the top corner, it's off the goalie's head, and that works for me too."

    a. True
    b. False

QUIZ ANSWERS

1. B – Real Chevrefils

2. A – True

3. C – Keith Crowder

4. D – $16 million

5. B – Don Marcotte

6. B – Wayne Gretzky

7. A – True

8. D – Brad Marchand

9. C – Modelling clothing in a series of shows for Boston designer Denise Hajjar

10. C – 8

11. A – High-rise building rigger

12. A – True

13. B – Chris Chelios

14. C – Maurice Richard

15. C – Rick Middleton

16. A – True

17. D – *Happy Gilmore*

18. A – Wayne Cashman

19. C – Pajamas

20. B – False

DID YOU KNOW?

1. Mark Recchi is one of just ten players in NHL history to win Stanley Cups with three teams. He triumphed with the 1991 Pittsburgh Penguins, 2006 Carolina Hurricanes, and 2011 Boston Bruins.

2. In an epic display of taunting, winger Johnny McKenzie created the "McKenzie Choke Dance," which he broke out after Boston defeated the New York Rangers for the 1972 Stanley Cup. McKenzie took center ice, put an arm up in a Statue of Liberty pose, placed a hand around his throat to simulate choking, and hopped around in a circle to torment the fans.

3. Two Bruins wingers, Woody Dumart and Bobby Bauer, joined their center Milt Schmidt as the first line mates to ever finish first, second, and third at the top of the NHL scoring race in 1939-40. In that low-scoring era, the trio combined for 138 points.

4. Woody Dumart was named for American president Woodrow Wilson. His full name was Woodrow Wilson Clarence Dumart. He was often called "Porky."

5. Fierce Boston left winger Milan Lucic, a Vancouver native, was so hated in his hometown after the Bruins defeated the Vancouver Canucks in the 2011 Stanley Cup Finals that his posters were defaced at a local community center, and his mere presence at a local festival incited a public brawl.

113

6. Great Bruins scouting led to the acquisition of undrafted free agent left winger Geoff Courtnall in 1983. Courtnall would make the team that fall, and though concussions cut short his career, he still achieved close to 800 points in over 1,000 career games. Not bad for an afterthought!

7. Bruins right wing/defenseman Dit Clapper played an incredible 20 seasons in the NHL. He holds the distinction of being the first player still alive at the time of his induction into the Hockey Hall of Fame, which occurred in 1947.

8. Former Bruins winger Ted Donato is the first ever NHL player to participate on the popular TV gameshow *The Price is Right*. He made it to the "Showcase Showdown" but lost when his bid on a harp, a satellite dish, and a boat was not close enough to the actual retail price.

9. Popular Bruin Cam Neely is one of only nine NHLers to achieve the difficult feat of scoring 50 goals in 50 games. He is the only Bruin to ever manage this, and the 44 games it took him to achieve it in 1993-94 are faster than any other player aside from Wayne Gretzky.

10. Anson Carter, a Bruin whose ancestry came from Barbados, founded his own hip hop record label, Big Up Entertainment, in 2005.

CHAPTER 14:

THE HEATED RIVALRIES

QUIZ TIME!

1. Which team have the Bruins most often matched up with in the playoffs?

   a. Toronto Maple Leafs
   b. Montreal Canadiens
   c. New York Rangers
   d. Detroit Red Wings

2. Boston leads the all-time series with the hated New York Rangers by over 50 wins.

   a. True
   b. False

3. In 1981, the Bruins set their franchise mark for most penalty minutes in a game, facing which opponent?

   a. Pittsburgh Penguins
   b. Toronto Maple Leafs
   c. Philadelphia Flyers
   d. Minnesota North Stars

4. How many consecutive games was Boston's longest winning streak against the Montreal Canadiens?

    a. 5
    b. 7
    c. 9
    d. 11

5. In more than one interview, Bruins great Cam Neely admitted to having "no respect" for which NHL defenseman?

    a. Chris Chelios
    b. Ulf Samuelsson
    c. Brad Park
    d. Scott Stevens

6. In the decade between 1982-1992, the Bruins and Sabres developed a rivalry by facing off against each other in five playoff series. How many of those did the Bruins win?

    a. 0
    b. 2
    c. 3
    d. 5

7. There is such animosity between Boston and Montreal that Boston police were once sent to the Canadiens' dressing room to arrest a player after a game between the two teams.

    a. True
    b. False

8. The first ever fight during an outdoor Winter Classic game took place when the Bruins played at Fenway Park in 2010. Who was their opponent?

   a. New York Islanders
   b. New York Rangers
   c. New Jersey Devils
   d. Philadelphia Flyers

9. In a chippy series in 2011, Vancouver's Aaron Rome drew the first ever multi-game suspension given out during a Stanley Cup Final. Which Bruin did he hit to receive this ban?

   a. Zdeno Chara
   b. Tim Thomas
   c. Nathan Horton
   d. Milan Lucic

10. The Bruins and Maple Leafs have played many tense playoff series. How long has it been since Toronto beat the Bruins in one of these playoff series?

   a. Over 15 years
   b. Over 30 years
   c. Over 45 years
   d. Over 60 years

11. Of which 1970s team did Bruins star Derek Sanderson say, "We hated them really. We thought they were complainers, whiners."?

   a. Chicago Blackhawks

b. New York Rangers

c. Philadelphia Flyers

d. Detroit Red Wings

12. Boston Bruins icon Ray Bourque despised the New Jersey Devils so much that he threatened to retire rather than be traded to them toward the end of his career.

a. True

b. False

13. This newer NHL squad considers Boston a potential major rival, based on recent competition to be the best in the Atlantic Division.

a. Ottawa Senators

b. Florida Panthers

c. Tampa Bay Lightning

d. Buffalo Sabres

14. During the Bruins 2019 Stanley Cup matchup against the St. Louis Blues, which two celebrities waged a social media rivalry in support of their hometown teams?

a. John Krasinski and Jenna Fischer

b. David Ortiz and Albert Pujols

c. Matt Damon and Jimmy Kimmel

d. Connor McGregor and Jon Hamm

15. Bruins legend Eddie Shore did not get along with the Montreal Maroons. How many fights did he engage in during one game against them in 1929 (setting the NHL record for single game bouts)?

a. 3

b. 4

c. 5

d. 6

16. Bruins trainers once tried to throw visiting Detroit Red Wings players off their game by leaving eight dead octopi rotting in their locker room.

a. True

b. False

17. Which NHL team's arena is geographically closest to Boston's?

a. New York Rangers

b. New Jersey Devils

c. Montreal Canadiens

d. New York Islanders

18. Bruins Hall-of-Famer Bobby Orr was known for his supreme skill, rather than his tendency to drop the gloves. Which player goaded Orr into more fights (3) than anyone else?

a. Vic Hadfield

b. Rosaire Paiement

c. Frank Mahovlich

d. Dennis Hextall

19. Multiple Bruins players, including Cam Neely and Marc Savard, have had their careers shortened or ended due to questionable hits by players from which team?

a. Los Angeles Kings

b. Anaheim Ducks

c. San Jose Sharks

d. Pittsburgh Penguins

20. The team with the most goals per game scored against the Bruins is the Colorado Avalanche.

a. True

b. False

QUIZ ANSWERS

1. B – Montreal Canadiens

2. A – True

3. D – Minnesota North Stars

4. C – 9

5. B – Ulf Samuelsson

6. D – 5

7. A – True

8. D – Philadelphia Flyers

9. C – Nathan Horton

10. D – Over 60 years

11. B – New York Rangers

12. B – False

13. C – Tampa Bay Lightning

14. A – John Krasinski and Jenna Fischer

15. C – 5

16. B – False

17. A – New York Rangers

18. B – Rosaire Paiement

19. D – Pittsburgh Penguins

20. A – True

DID YOU KNOW?

1. In a game against Montreal in 1955, Bruins defenseman Hal Laycoe high-sticked Maurice "Rocket" Richard in the head. Richard received five stitches, returned to the ice, broke his stick over Laycoe's body, and then twice punched the referee who was trying to contain the violence. His resulting suspension led to riots in the streets of Montreal.

2. Fifty-nine years later, in 2014, tensions between the Bruins and Habs still ran high. After the Habs defeated the Bruins in Game 7 of their playoff series, Bruins forward Milan Lucic skated through the traditional handshake line and told Canadiens player Dale Weise, "I'm going to kill you next year."

3. The Bruins vs. Maple Leafs rivalry took off in 1933, when Boston's Eddie Shore checked Toronto's Ace Bailey from behind, sending him onto the ice and fracturing his skull. Bailey never played again and was the first player whose number was retired by any team.

4. Boston strikes fear in the hearts of Toronto fans as a playoff opponent. Three times during the 2010s, Boston has edged Toronto in a seventh, and deciding game, including 2013, when they sent Toronto home in heartbreak after the Bruins rallied from a 4-1 deficit in the third period to come back for a triumphant overtime victory.

5. High quality hockey was at the genesis of the Bruins rivalry with the Philadelphia Flyers. Both teams won two Stanley Cups in the 1970s, and they faced each other in three consecutive semifinal matchups, with the Bruins taking two of the three.

6. Without much history between them, Boston and Vancouver did not seem likely to develop much of a rivalry when they met in the 2011 Stanley Cup Finals. But when Vancouver's Alex Burrows bit the finger of Boston star Patrice Bergeron during a scrum, the series became heated to the point where Vancouver fans rioted in the streets after the Bruins won the Cup.

7. Rivalries are usually based on even competition, but Boston has been so good that they only have losing records against 4 of the other 30 NHL franchises (Detroit, Minnesota, Anaheim, and Montreal).

8. On December 13, 1972, Boston forward Wayne Cashman tangled with Jim Schoenfeld of the Sabres. The two collided so vigorously that they burst through the Zamboni doors. Rather than return to the ice, the two decided to fight in the tunnel while linesmen tried in vain to break it up.

9. The 2011 Bruins had not won the Stanley Cup in 39 long years. Facing Montreal in the playoffs, they won three games in overtime, including Game 4, in which Andrew Ference scored a goal. Ference promptly turned to the Montreal crowd and flipped them the middle finger. The

Bruins would end their draught and become champions later that year.

10. Bitter rivals rarely trade with each other, but on November 7, 1975, the Bruins swapped emotional leader Phil Esposito with the New York Rangers for Jean Ratelle and Brad Park. Esposito was devastated and said, "It took me probably a year to accept that I wasn't part of the Boston Bruins anymore."

CHAPTER 15:

THE AWARDS SECTION

QUIZ TIME!

1. The NHL has given out the Mark Messier Leadership Award since 2006. Who has been the only Bruin to win it?

    a. Patrice Bergeron

    b. Zdeno Chara

    c. Tim Thomas

    d. Torey Krug

2. The Bruins have won the Presidents' Trophy (for most points in a regular season) at least once in every decade of their existence.

    a. True

    b. False

3. Who was the most recent Boston forward to make the NHL All-Rookie Team?

    a. Joe Juneau

    b. Sergei Samsonov

    c. David Pastrnak

    d. Brad Boyes

4. Which of these Bruins mainstays has never won an Art Ross Trophy as the league's leading scorer?

   a. Phil Esposito
   b. Milt Schmidt
   c. Ray Bourque
   d. Bobby Orr

5. The Bruins are the last team to produce back-to-back rookies who won the Calder Trophy. Which players accomplished the feat for them?

   a. Cam Neely and Ray Bourque
   b. Sergei Samsonov and Joe Thornton
   c. Andrew Raycroft and Glen Murray
   d. Bobby Orr and Derek Sanderson

6. Phil Kessel is one of four Boston players to win the Bill Masterton Trophy for resilience and dedication to hockey; the other three players received it after suffering hockey injuries. What did Kessel overcome before receiving it?

   a. Testicular cancer
   b. Bipolar disorder
   c. Diabetes
   d. Third-degree burns

7. Noted pest Brad Marchand inspired the creation of a new award, the Esa Tikkanen Trophy, for the player who "most gets under the skin" of opposing teams each year.

   a. True
   b. False

8. Of the many Bruins in the Hockey Hall of Fame, Sprague Cleghorn is first among them to skate with the Bruins. What year did he begin playing with the team?

    a. 1922
    b. 1924
    c. 1925
    d. 1928

9. Eddie Shore captured the Hart Trophy (for league's most valuable player) four times, more than any other Bruin. Where does he rank on the league-wide list for most Hart wins of all time?

    a. 1st
    b. 7th
    c. 10th
    d. 3rd

10. In 2000, the Bruins created an award to honor their great forward Johnny Bucyk. What is this award given for?

    a. Best performance in the shootout
    b. Charity work in the community
    c. Penalty killing excellence
    d. Most revered by teammates

11. Goaltender Tiny Thompson won four Vezina Trophies (for best goaltender in the league) with the Bruins between 1929-1938. What was Tiny's real first name?

    a. Cecil
    b. Lawrence

c. Thomas

d. Archibald

12. No Bruin has ever won a gold medal at the Winter Olympics.

   a. True

   b. False

13. Which Bruins player has been selected to the most NHL All-Star Games?

   a. Eddie Shore

   b. Johnny Bucyk

   c. Frank Brimsek

   d. Ray Bourque

14. In which decade did the Boston Bruins NOT have a coach win the Jack Adams Award (for top coach) during the regular season?

   a. 1970s

   b. 1980s

   c. 1990s

   d. 2000s

15. How many Boston Bruins have been elected to the Hall of Fame in the "Builder" category?

   a. 0

   b. 3

   c. 6

   d. 9

16. Bruins players have won more Norris Trophies (for the NHL's best defenseman) than any other team.

    a. True
    b. False

17. Boston has won six Stanley Cup championships, but has only three players who have won a Conn Smythe Trophy (for most valuable player in the playoffs), why?

    a. The trophy was awarded to a player from another team whose performance stood out despite his team's loss.
    b. The trophy was not in existence yet when some of those Cups were won.
    c. Some Bruins players have won the trophy more than once.
    d. A Bruins player declined to accept the trophy to show solidarity with teammates.

18. What was the only year in which the original Boston Garden hosted an NHL All-Star Game?

    a. 1961
    b. 1991
    c. 1981
    d. 1971

19. How many teams have more Stanley Cup championships than the six that the Boston Bruins possess?

    a. 2
    b. 3

c. 4

d. 5

20. Two Bruins broadcasters, Fred Cusick and Bob Wilson, have won the Foster Hewitt Memorial Award (for contributions to hockey and broadcasting).

a. True

b. False

QUIZ ANSWERS

1. B – Zdeno Chara

2. B – False

3. D – Brad Boyes

4. C – Ray Bourque

5. D – Bobby Orr and Derek Sanderson

6. A – Testicular cancer

7. B – False

8. C – 1925

9. D – 3rd

10. B – Charity work in the community

11. A – Cecil

12. B – False

13. D – Ray Bourque

14. B – 1980s

15. C – 6

16. A – True

17. B – The trophy was not in existence yet when some of those Cups were won.

18. D – 1971

19. B – 3

20. A – True

DID YOU KNOW?

1. When the NHL season ends, the Bruins sponsor a fan vote each year for the Seventh Player Award, which is given to someone who "performed beyond expectations." Ed Westfall was the first winner, in 1968.

2. Two players born in Massachusetts have gone on to play for the Bruins AND be elected to the United States Hockey Hall of Fame. They are Mike Milbury and Bill Guerin.

3. Each year, the Bruins give out their own Eddie Shore Award, which goes to the player who best exemplifies hustle and work ethic over the course of the season.

4. The team known as "The Big, Bad Bruins" has nonetheless managed to pick up eight Lady Byng Memorial Trophies, which are given to the sport's most gentlemanly player. Right winger Bobby Bauer led the way with three.

5. Bobby Orr's 1970 season was so dominant that he won both the Lionel Conacher Award (for top male athlete in all of Canada) AND the Lou Marsh Trophy (for best Canadian athlete). Two years later, Phil Esposito repeated the feat.

6. In the 1930s, before the All-Star Game was created, the NHL chose players to play in benefit games to raise funds for the families of players who had suffered misfortunes or died. Three such games were held, and Boston's Eddie

Shore played in all three, while Dit Clapper suited up for two.

7. Tuukka Rask has been a mainstay in the Bruins' net and has won the Vezina Trophy as the league's best goaltender, but he has never won the William M. Jennings Trophy for fewest goals given up in the regular season.

8. The Elizabeth C. Dufresne Trophy is given out to the player who performs the best in Boston's home games. Ray Bourque tops the list of winners, having taken home the award seven times.

9. Former Boston player Don Sweeney worked his way up to becoming the general manager of the Bruins after his retirement. In 2019, he became the team's first winner of the NHL's Jim Gregory General Manager of the Year Award.

10. Two Bruins have won the Golden Hockey Stick, given annually to the best Czech hockey player. David Krejci was the first to win, and David Pastrnak has won it three times consecutively.

CONCLUSION

There you have it; an amazing collection of Bruins trivia, information, and statistics at your fingertips! Regardless of how you fared on the quizzes, we hope you found this book entertaining, enlightening, and educational.

Ideally, you knew many of these details, but also learned a good deal more about the history of the Boston Bruins, their players, coaches, management, and some of the quirky stories surrounding the team. If you got a little peek into the colorful details that make being a fan so much more enjoyable, then mission accomplished!

The good news is the trivia doesn't have to stop there! Spread the word. Challenge your fellow Bruins fans to see if they can do any better. Share some of the stories with the next generation to help them become Boston supporters too.

If you are a big enough Bruins fan, consider creating your own quiz with some of the details you know that weren't presented here, and then test your friends to see if they can match your knowledge.

The Boston Bruins are a storied franchise. They have a long history, with many periods of success, and a few that were less than successful. They've had glorious superstars, iconic moments, hilarious tales...but most of all, they have wonderful, passionate fans. Thank you for being one of them.

Made in United States
North Haven, CT
25 July 2023

39521827R00078